Being a Catholic
GRANDMOTHER

redemptorist
publications

Contents

Catherine thanks Pope Francis for all he is doing to honour and empower grandparents in their vocation to pass on the faith.

Foreword

Our mission: *"To help grandparents pass on the faith, to value and support them in that role and keep prayer at the heart of family life."*

In September 2001 I was at Mass in Walsingham, in the medieval Slipper Chapel of Our Lady. While there, I began to wonder what I could give the Blessed Virgin Mary for her birthday; what would truly delight her? I had the idea of a grandparents' pilgrimage to honour and thank her parents, Saints Joachim and Anne, for all they had done – particularly in the formation of the faith. I had recently become a grandmother myself, and although it was full of joy, it was not everything I thought it would be. I became aware that it was a great responsibility.

On 26 July 2002, on the feast of Ss Joachim and Anne, the inaugural Grandparents' Pilgrimage was held in Walsingham. It was a day full of faith, fun, graces and blessings. We could never have imagined how these pilgrimages would delight Our Lady, but clearly they did, as the Grandparents' Pilgrimage spread from Walsingham in the East of England to Knock in Ireland. Before long there were pilgrimages and Masses celebrated all over the world – in England, Scotland, America, Australia, Malta, Gibraltar, Portugal, Slovenia, Slovakia, Poland, Tanzania, Cambodia and Nigeria.

In 2008 Pope Benedict XVI composed the *Universal Prayer for Grandparents* at the request of the Catholic Grandparents' Association. This has since been translated into many languages. In 2012 we held the tenth national Grandparents' Pilgrimage in Walsingham, and the sixth in Knock. Up to twelve thousand people now attend the Knock pilgrimage each year. In 2009 all these initiatives converged when the Catholic Grandparents' Association was officially launched in Knock, at a gathering of fourteen thousand people. It is growing organically – so clearly there is a need.

Grandparents are beginning to realise that they need something to bridge the gap and to pass on the faith to a lost generation before it is too late. To support them, the Association organises events, seminars, workshops, prayer appeals and television appearances, and produces resources for grandparents. Many of the events involve the family directly. For example, the annual Children's Prayer Appeal involves children writing beautiful prayers for their grandparents; while the grandparents' days in schools involve grandparents meeting children and teachers to share their own growing-up experiences. The Association also organises the "Adopt-a-Prayer-Child" scheme, whereby a grandparent in a nursing or care home prays for a sick grandchild, and the child's family in turn prays for the grandparent.

Pilgrimages are the mainstay of everything that we do. To my mind they are a fitting combination of family and faith, with grandparents as their focus. They are empowering, enabling, joyful celebrations. It is always inspiring to see grandparents attending with their grandchildren, supported by their family. It was John Paul II who said that "Pilgrimages to shrines of Our Lady are the natural place for families to go to give thanks and to find their identity".

In addition, there is a campaigning element to the Association's work. In a bid to get the role of grandparenting recognised and respected, the President, Maire Printer, and I have travelled the world, presenting our work at conferences, workshops and at meetings with church representatives. We use every opportunity to create awareness of the vital contribution grandparents can make to the Church, to the family and to society. By God's grace we believe the Church is paying more attention,

and that the Church recognises the need to support grandparents while they are supporting everyone else.

I neither consider myself a holy person, nor do I feel worthy of this great task that God and Our Lady have blessed me with – a job I will never retire from. But I am absolutely passionate about promoting awareness for the great vocation of grandparents. Above all, I am convinced that grandparents' prayers are very powerful, and that a loving grandparent can do absolutely anything.

Being a Catholic Grandmother is an important and useful resource because it reminds us that grandparents should have no agenda. We simply want the best for our grandchildren. We want them to be good, decent human-beings who know the difference between right and wrong and are able to make good, moral decisions. And if our grandchildren do go astray along the way, we want them to be able to find their way back to a loving, forgiving, non-judgemental God.

May our Holy Mother Mary, the Holy Spirit and the love of Jesus continue to guide and inspire us.

Catherine Wiley,
founder of the Catholic Grandparents' Association

Introduction

You may be a relatively young woman setting out on the great adventure of grandmotherhood, or you may have several grandchildren – who may be babies, toddlers, children, teenagers or adults.

You may be retired, or working part-time or full-time. You may care for your grandchild or have other family responsibilities, such as looking after parents or even grandparents of your own. You might be in a relationship, married, widowed, divorced, separated, or none of the above. All of these things are perfectly possible – and none of them should exclude you from enjoying grandmotherhood to the full!

Similarly, your relationship with your grandchild will depend on your circumstances. Undoubtedly your relationship with your own child and his or her family will be an influencing factor. That may be affected by geography – whether you live near your extended family or on opposite sides of the world. You might be a grandmother (or even great-grandmother) to other children. Then there is the sometimes thorny issue of family relationships: you may feel a welcome part of the family, or relations might be tricky – even to the point that you feel ostracised and discouraged, or you are denied access to your grandchild. Thankfully these are rare scenarios, but if this strikes a chord you are by no means alone.

In addition, your own faith story will be as unique as your thumbprint. You may be a "cradle Catholic" and lifelong churchgoer, or – and this is not at all uncommon – it is possible that the experience of grandmotherhood has reconnected you with your faith (what a wonderful testament to the transformative power of birth). Similarly, your child and their family may be practising Catholics, or they may have moved away from the faith.

Given the sheer scope of grandmotherhood, it would be impossible to produce a "one-size-fits-all" guide. Rather, the aim of this book is to share the ups and downs that many grandmothers experience, and to offer ideas on how to enjoy the good times and cope with the bad. Some of the illustrations may strike a chord, while others might even provoke a pang of envy or regret. For example, there are references to childbirth and "the parents", but the intention is certainly not to marginalise or exclude single-parent families, or those where a child or grandchild is adopted.

The rich diversity of families – with all their ups and downs, advantages and drawbacks – is part of God's wonderful creation. So pray for wisdom and insight. If you discover, while in prayer, that something really is wrong, pray that God reveals how you can address it. But if you find that it is simply a case that you do not fit the conventional family mould, pray that God helps you to relax, enjoy and celebrate your uniqueness.

Your individuality as a woman is God-given, and your family and faith are unique to you. However, you do have something in common with all grandmothers around the world: you have given rise to two generations of human beings. It is sometimes easy to lose sight of just what an awesome achievement that is. So whatever your story, it is hoped that this guide will help you to use the rich experience of grandmotherhood to find your way to a deeper faith, and to connect you and your family more strongly with the Church, which provides the infrastructure, support and continuity for your faith.

Above all, this book is designed to help you to discover a deeper sense of God's presence in your growing relationship with your grandchildren and in your evolving relationship with your own children. As one ecstatic grandmother said, "If I had known how fantastic grandchildren are, I would have had them first!"

 7

Catherine's top tips

Take some time to reflect and pray about your own relationship with your parents and grandparents.

▶ How did they help you on your journey to adult faith?

▶ What is your first memory of your grandparents?

▶ What do you consider to be the most important message that you can impart to your own grandchildren?

Share what you discover with other grandparents and find out their stories as well.

"Granny talks to me about God and she says the world is bigger than what I can see."

Joel, age 7

Chapter one

A new identity

Let us assume for a moment that you are a first-time grandmother. If you are not, just backtrack to the birth of your first grandchild and remember how you heard about it. What was your first response and how did you feel at that first meeting? Probably, like so many grandmothers, you felt a renewed sense of wonder and overwhelming love and peace at the reality of the birth.

That moment marks a deep change in you, as well as your newborn grandchild. There are now three generations instead of two, and you have shifted to a new place in the family tree. As your status changes from mother to grandmother, you are presented with a whole new set of challenges, unique to your individual circumstances. While some women are ready to be grandmothers, this new identity does not sit easily for everyone, and it can take time to get used to the idea of being a grandmother – so go easy on yourself. Recognise the enormity of what has happened and its impact on you, then give this new experience time to settle into your heart, your daily life and your faith life. Above all, pray – and keep praying – for God's guidance over the coming days, weeks, months and years.

Prayer to greet a newborn baby

Lord, as we welcome a new life into the world, and prepare to accompany this blessed child on (his, her) faith journey, grant that we may be born anew ourselves, to see the world through fresh eyes. Allow this birth, Lord, to touch our hearts with joy. Amen.

Help! Where is the rule book for grandmothers?

You probably remember how each stage of your baby's development presented you with a new challenge. Do you recall the anxiety of watching anything and everything move from their hand to their mouth? Or how you would constantly scan the room for potential hazards when they reached the crawling and toddling stage? You will doubtless remember how extremely tiring it was having to be relentlessly vigilant, needing to have "eyes in the back of your head", or fretting about how he or she would cope with school and first friendships – not to mention the emotional minefields of adolescence, puberty and the excruciating teenage years.

At each of these stages, your challenge was to find the balance between letting them explore the world for themselves – making the occasional mistake – and protecting them from serious harm. The new challenge of grandmotherhood is learning how to do this all over again – but at one remove. So it is not a task to be underestimated; neither is it one you can opt out of, as you are committed from the moment you hear the words, "We've got something to tell you…"

The encouraging thing is that you learnt nearly all the skills you need the first time round. Yes, you might be rusty and you might not have changed a nappy in decades, but have faith – it will come back to you when you need it. Do you remember an occasion when that powerful mother's instinct kicked in and you "just knew" something was awry? These are the gifts that God gives every mother. The amazing thing is that God revives them in grandmothers as well.

> "I was ambushed by my emotional reactions to becoming a grandmother. Never had it occurred to me that I would, through my grandchildren, rediscover, revisit, relive the love I felt for my own children when they were babies… I have never been so conscious of, and grateful for, the rhythm of life."
>
> Miriam Stoppard,
> *doctor and writer*

Learning to let go

Your maternal instincts and skills may have survived intact, but there is an additional challenge for new grandmothers – namely how to love so powerfully, from a distance.

Cast your mind back to the moments after the birth of your child. Remember that tiny form being placed in your arms, and against your breast, as though it was still part of your body, utterly dependent on you for food, warmth and shelter. The chances are that you were so totally wrapped up in that moment that every scrap of love and attention was poured into your newborn. Well that tiny form has now grown and is going through an experience similar to the one you had.

For many women, the challenge of grandmotherhood is judging when and how to give the parents hands-on support, when to play a supporting role, and when to back off completely. It should never be underestimated what strength of emotion it can provoke.

One of the hardest things to let go of can be the urge to impart your Catholic faith to your grandchildren, particularly if your own child has moved away from the faith. As we shall explore in this book, it can be extremely upsetting to realise – to use an example – that your grandchild is not going to be baptised. One rule, which is worth emphasising from the outset, is:

TRY NOT to forcibly pass on the faith to your grandchildren if their parents have told you not to.

You will be found out and it will only lead to resentment. In extreme cases, it could result in you being given limited access to your grandchild.

> **"Faith, as the saying has it, is more caught than taught. The best we can do with our grandchildren is the same thing we did for our children: expose them and trust God to do the rest."**
>
> Carol Luebering,
> *author*

Even if at times you have to bite your tongue, do not undervalue the importance of your role to be a force for good in the life – and faith life – of your grandchild. This is something Pope Benedict XVI touched on when he composed the *Prayer for Grandparents* in 2008. In it he called grandparents "living treasures of sound religious traditions". If that sounds like a lot to live up to, take heart and remember, this is not something you have to become, it is who you are already! So if you enter into grandmotherhood with an open heart and open arms, alive with faith and prayer, and supported by your church community, you will find that you are very well equipped to meet this awesome challenge head on – and that the rewards of doing so are beyond words.

"Granny listens to me, and she doesn't have huge ears or anything."

Beth, age 5

Chapter two

Sharing the Church's values

We often hear that the number of people who regularly attend church is declining. However, by God's grace, the Church is thriving in many corners of the world.

If your family is part of that, enjoy it to the full: thank God for every prayer you say together, every time you stand side by side at Mass, or kneel together at the altar rail. Also thank God for the harmony of your voices singing together and for every sacrament you share.

But make a clear distinction between feeling proud and being smug. Jesus frequently spoke about the importance of being vigilant (for example, Matthew 24:42). Your calling is to ensure that your family's faith life never becomes a dull routine or empty duty, but instead stays vibrant and alive. How you go about this depends on what you do already, but here are some ideas:

▶ Encourage discussion and lively debate about faith. In other words, do not allow it to become a taboo subject. Try to encourage people to share their real feelings, including doubts and concerns. Keep the conversation going until it is an everyday topic of discussion.

▶ Do you ever do any charity work as a family, or take part in church activities? If that is not the kind of thing you do, give some thought as to why not.

Prayer for a safe journey

Lord, who has brought us together as a family today, keep [Name] and [Name] safe on their journey home, and grant us many more wonderful times together.
Amen.

▶ Arrange a visit to a church, cathedral, shrine or even a religious community. You will be amazed how fascinating children and young people find religious life. Many communities are open to visits, providing you make advance arrangements. Read up on it beforehand to make it as interesting as possible.

▶ Could you pray more often? If you say grace before meals when the family visits, how about a brief prayer when they leave?

▶ It is rare for all members of a family to stay firm in faith. Ask yourself, is anyone struggling?

▶ Is there anything you could do to help strengthen the faith life of another family?

Catherine's top tips

You may think that you need to know a lot about theology to teach anything to your grandchildren, but, in fact, you know most of it already, and learning with a grandchild can be a rare joy. Here are some ideas to help you pass on the Catholic faith to your grandchild:

▶ Read a children's Bible. Children love the stories of Moses, the good Samaritan, and David and Goliath.

▶ Explain, in simple terms, the significance of Christmas and Easter.

▶ Say grace before meals. Your grandchild will soon learn the words and will eventually recite them with you.

▶ Teach your grandchild simple prayers like "Prayer to a guardian angel", the "Our Father", and "Hail Mary".

▶ Encourage your grandchild to recite a classic bedtime prayer, such as "Now I lay me down to sleep".

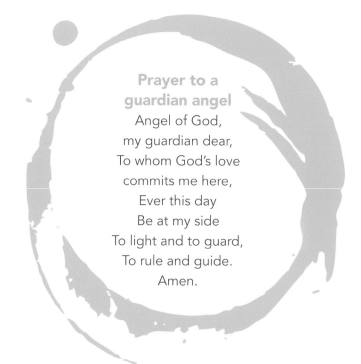

Prayer to a guardian angel
Angel of God,
my guardian dear,
To whom God's love
commits me here,
Ever this day
Be at my side
To light and to guard,
To rule and guide.
Amen.

Faith no more

If your family is one of the many being challenged by a disruption to the continuity of faith, it can be upsetting to realise that the break comes between you and the generation immediately following you. It is hard not to feel personally responsible. Of course it is not a phenomenon limited to your family. It is part of a wider, cultural process of secularisation. As a grandmother trying to bridge the generation gap, with the faith you hold so close to your heart, do not underestimate the enormity of the task – and do not shirk from it either! Pray for the courage and resources to meet it head on.

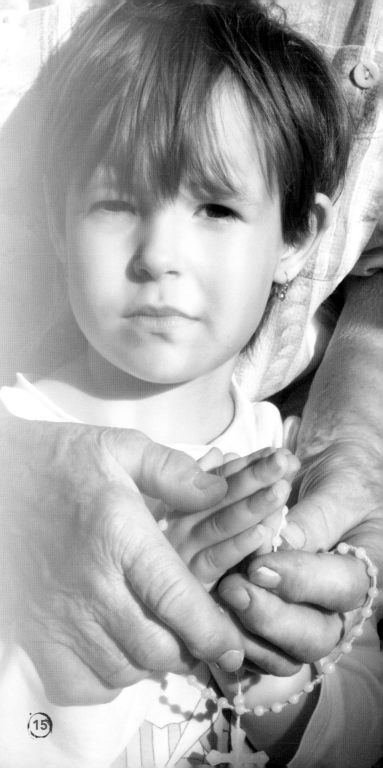

There is the idea that parents whose children turn away from the faith must have done something wrong. But as you will probably have witnessed in friends and family, attending Mass every Sunday, saying grace before every meal and reading the Bible regularly does not guarantee that your children will grow up to be practising Catholics.

Parents cannot predict the kind of adults their children will become in any respect; it is part of the marvellous but unnerving mystery that is parenthood. Then again, God works in wonderful and mysterious ways. You may know someone whose child became resolutely anti-Catholic for a while, before turning back to the faith. When someone embraces faith as an adult, it is often a deep and lasting commitment. If your enthusiasm for Catholicism is not welcomed or encouraged, possibly even to the point where you feel unable to mention God, it might help to think of your role as akin to that of the Church. Like the Church, you – simply by being who you are – are able to give your family a sense of connection in terms of place, history and Catholic heritage. And, again like the Church, sometimes all you can do is just be there, be yourself and make it clear that you are ready to talk when the time is right.

Chapter three

Accompanying your grandchild *through the ages*

In this section we look at the stages of childhood and the teenage years. We also review the sacraments that typically accompany each stage, and ask how a grandmother's relationship with her grandchild might develop.

Baby LOVE

Everyone crowds around a newborn baby. It is such a powerful human instinct – a real physical craving – to be as close as possible to this little miracle. The experience of grandmotherhood can reignite the maternal instinct in a very powerful way and it can feel almost physically painful to resist the urge to completely wrap yourself around your grandchild. But parents, uncles, aunts, brothers, sisters and other grandparents all have a claim on this new addition to the family – so at times you must resist. When your grandchild is prised from your reluctant arms and passed to someone else, say a silent prayer to acknowledge the awesome power of this bond. Also, thank God that your grandchild is surrounded by so much love, and by people who will nurture and protect him or her throughout their life.

Some grandmothers really struggle with this, so here are a few coping strategies:

▶ Try to remember the emotional and physical upheavals you went through after childbirth and relate that to what the parents are experiencing.

▶ If you know another grandmother you can confide in, arrange to meet for a coffee and share your feelings with her.

▶ A very therapeutic exercise is to create a grandparents' book with prayers, poems, hymns, snippets of history and photos of you and other family members. The possibilities are endless, and there will come a day when you can share them with your grandchild.

Catherine's top tip

Do you have any idea how many deep family divisions occur over the name of a grandchild? A name, as Shakespeare once said, is just a name. So try to avoid falling into the trap of playing the "name game"!

Baptism

While desperate to know the answer, many grandparents are too afraid to ask their children if their baby is going to be baptised. It is important to remember that baptism is an expression of your son or daughter's faith – not your own. You did your bit when you had your own child baptised.

Assuming that baptism is on the cards, this is a good opportunity to create or strengthen links with your extended family, as someone now exists in the world whose genetic makeup is a mixture of your family and another one.

Do not be surprised or dismayed if you feel a strong resistance to being connected with another family who may be, after all, essentially strangers. We are naturally reserved creatures and we can be guilty at times of "ring-fencing" our families and treating outsiders as intruders. So if you recognise these tendencies in yourself, remember that the other family may also be going through something similar – so why not meet them with an open heart?

Watch out for pride or snobbery and, above all, try not to allow your natural reserve to suck you into competitive game-playing or rivalry. Remember that at the centre of this is your grandchild, who will ultimately benefit from a strong support network on all sides.

Do:

▶ whatever it takes to develop the relationship. If appropriate, contact the other grandmother to ask what she is wearing to the ceremony, or to consult on what gifts you are both buying for the baby.

▶ offer to provide refreshments for the reception, if it is appropriate. But remember that the greater humility might lie in letting someone else do it, or in sharing the workload.

Don't:

▶ do anything to encourage or exacerbate competitive tendencies in other family members.

▶ force yourself to like anyone else. If you simply do not "gel", pray for compassion and understanding. But accept that you may never become best friends.

Toddling along

During your grandchild's toddler years you will be an invaluable source of help and support to the parents. You may be in the privileged position of being able to provide regular day care, occasional babysitting, an overnight stay, a weekend, or even longer. But bear in mind that the "terrible twos" can be a very taxing period and it is wise, before agreeing to anything, to give careful thought to what is manageable.

Of course you want to help out, particularly when childcare costs are so high. Furthermore, if you regularly visited or stayed with your own grandparents as a child, you probably remember it as a magical time – something you would like to replicate for your own grandchild. But you probably never had the slightest inkling how much work it involved for your grandparents, or the scale of disruption that you caused their home life! What is more, the chances are that you lead a much busier life than your grandmother did, so do not be hard on yourself if you are not able to offer as much support as you would like. Remember, if you are overstretched and stressed, the hours you spend with your grandchild will not be quality time.

Ruth writes:

Our daughter and her husband have two beautiful children: Felix, aged four, and Maddie, aged one. Our daughter has just returned to full-time work and I have the kids two days a week. I work part-time as well. I love having them, but if I am honest, I find it hard to cope with the mess. In fact, it is really getting me down. In the twenty-six years since I had anything to do with toddlers, I have become used to a very clean and tidy house, and sometimes it feels like pure anarchy when the kids are over. The other day Maddie dropped her food, and the minute I cleared it up I found Felix had taken a pen and drawn all over our new wallpaper. I just erupted, which made him cry. I felt so awful. After spending the whole day with my grandchildren I am absolutely shattered, I become grumpy with my husband, and I feel exhausted at work the following day. Please help as I am worried that I cannot be the grandmother I want to be.

P.T.O. for Catherine's reply

Catherine replies:

Dear Ruth,

There is no universal advice on how to approach this, other than to say you are certainly not alone! I meet many grandmothers who run themselves ragged trying to help their children. So the first thing to say is do not feel bad if part of you resents these visits – it is understandable.

Secondly, reading between the lines, I would say you are putting on a brave face and suffering in silence. You probably remember how tiring it is to be a young parent, and naturally you want to take the pressure off your daughter and son-in-law. Also, the last thing you want to do is burden them with your own problems. But if it pushes you to exhaustion you will be no good to anyone. So talk to your daughter. Be clear that you love having the grandchildren round; but let her know that as things stand, it is taking too great a toll on you.

Thirdly, if you want to go on helping with childcare two days a week, you will need some help. Just a bit may make all the difference. Could the person who picks up the kids spend five minutes helping you to clear up? Could your husband help out? Or are you in a position to take on a cleaner? It sounds as though you have become used to being in control of your home. So I suggest you treat this as a lesson in relinquishing control, and please do not underestimate how hard that can be!

Lastly, when you have a bit of time, sit down with the Bible and read about Martha and Mary (Luke 10:38-42). Then, when you next have the kids, practise being less of "a Martha" and more of "a Mary". For half an hour (set a timer if it helps) try to forget the spaghetti on the floor and scribbles on the wall, and focus on spending quality time with Felix and Maddie.
God bless you and your family.

Catherine

> "Nobody can do for little children what grandparents do. Grandparents sort of sprinkle stardust over the lives of little children."

Alex Haley, author of *Roots: The Saga of an American Family*

Catherine's top tips

Make sure your home is baby safe: check locks, cupboard doors (particularly on low cupboards that contain household detergents), other doors, stairs and plugs. Also, make sure water (for example, a pond) is fenced off, and cables and blind cords are out of reach. See p.63 for a list of websites featuring child safety resources.

Discuss with your grandchild's parents any measures you have taken, so they feel safe leaving their children with you.

"If God is like grandma, then I think I'm OK!"

Alfie, age 6

The school years

The summer is winding down and your grandchild is heading to school for the first time. This transition to the classroom can bring about many anxieties for young children. They may wonder, "Will I make friends? "What if I can't do the work?" Such thoughts can make children extremely nervous before that "first day". Even if you are not on the frontline, it is important to recognise how you can support your grandchild at the beginning of the school year.

As a grandparent, you have the advantage of wisdom and experience. Therefore, consider what you can teach and share to help him or her to become mentally prepared for the school year ahead.

"Telling off" your grandchild

This is a good skill for a grandparent to learn. For one thing, you can be an extremely useful ally to a parent – "When granny tells us off we know it's really serious." So make it clear that you mean it, as mixed messages are never helpful. Jesus knew better than anyone how to rebuke with love – always clear and direct, but never unkind or unfair. For an example, turn to Mark 8:33 to read how he rebukes Peter.

Do:

▶ learn the rules laid down by the parents, and work within them.

▶ feel entitled to set boundaries within your own home, and let the parents know what they are.

Catherine's **top tip**

Agree with the parents what the consequences of bad behaviour should be, and enforce the punishment.

"My Gran wisely held that there are two kinds of spoiling: the good kind and the bad kind. When I got into trouble, I always fled to her room. I knew she would not come to my defence or criticise my mother – she never did. She just let me sit with her. All the while, I soaked up the reassurance that, however wicked I might be, I was still lovable. That was spoiling par excellence."

Carol Luebering,
author

A prayer to say with a child starting school

Lord, as [Name] starts school, we ask you to go with (him, her) into the classroom.
Help (him, her) to make good friends and to be fair and kind to all (his, her) classmates.
Guide [Name] as (he, she) works hard and is a good student for (his, her) teachers.
Amen.

Stephanie writes:

A teacher took my son aside recently and told him that my eight-year-old granddaughter Leah had been spiteful to another little girl at school – not just once, but several times. At first I could not believe it because she is such a sweet angel. But my son and daughter-in-law persuaded me that it was true. Whenever they bring up the subject with Leah, she just gets furious and will not talk about it. So they have asked me to talk to her. We have always been very close, so how can I ensure that she does not turn against me as well?

P.T.O. for Catherine's reply

Catherine replies:

Dear Stephanie

It sounds as though you have a very special relationship with this little girl. Naturally you are afraid of doing anything to jeopardise eight years of trust. But on the other hand, it is good to move your relationship forward – and what an honour it is that her parents trust you to take care of such an important task! I suggest you use a softly-softly approach. Do you ever read with her? If so, choose stories from a child's Bible that feature people who treat others badly. You could read the story of Joseph and his brothers (Genesis 37), before moving on to the good Samaritan (Luke 10:29-37). The latter gives an example of kindness. Encourage Leah to recognise the contrasting behaviours and to think about how it would feel to be the victim of bullying and spite. Your ultimate aim is to teach her the lesson of Matthew 7:12: "… treat others as you would like them to treat you."

If the stories encourage her to confess, that is a big breakthrough. Acknowledging our wrongdoings is a huge step in the right direction.

Lastly, I would like to share a story of my own with you, which you may find helpful. I recently heard my daughter Francesca talking to her nine-year-old son, Tom, who had obviously told a lie, but would not admit it. I heard Francesca say, "Tom, what is your little voice saying to you?"

What a great moral lesson for a mother to teach her son. I was so proud of her!

My prayers are with you and both families.

Catherine

Reconciliation and First Holy Communion

Busy parents may be more than grateful if you offer to help prepare your grandchild for first confession and First Holy Communion.

It is the duty of parents and those who take their place, as it is the duty of the parish priest, to ensure that before a child takes their First Holy Communion he or she has already been baptised, has made their sacramental confession and has enough knowledge to be able to receive the Body of Christ with faith and devotion.

If you are going to take on this important responsibility, here are some things to consider:

Teaching the Sacrament of Reconciliation

The first thing to emphasise is that this is not about listing our sins and misdemeanours. It is instead a way of making things better between ourselves, other people and God. Before your grandchild can celebrate the Sacrament of Reconciliation, he or she must prepare themselves by examining their conscience. Here are a few questions you can help your grandchild to consider before they make their first confession:

▶ Reflection: What did Jesus teach me?

▶ Examination: What am I sorry for?

▶ Confession: What do I want to tell the priest?

▶ Forgiveness: What will I do differently once God forgives me?

▶ Sharing: Who else can I say sorry to?

Do:

▶ discuss with the parents, a catechist or the parish priest your plans for helping to prepare your grandchild for their first confession and First Holy Communion. This will help to avoid duplication and will ensure that you do not contradict one another.

▶ consult your parish catechist or priest as they will be able to suggest appropriate reading material.

▶ plan a catechetical session with your grandchild. Set aside the time (you may find that half an hour is plenty at first) and find a quiet place where you can both think, talk and pray. If you are going to read a Bible story, decide in advance and prepare any books or materials that you will need (pens, paper etc.). Remember to be clear about what you would like your grandchild to get out of the session.

▶ introduce your grandchild to prayer and encourage him or her to pray for others.

▶ write up a few simple notes after each session and be prepared to share what you have been doing with the parents, parish priest, etc.

Catherine's top tip

Play board games with your grandchildren – especially games like *snakes and ladders* and *draughts*. They are good antidotes to television and can teach valuable lessons about patience, and winning and losing. But do not be tempted to let the children win every time!

Don't:

▶ tell your grandchild what to confess. He or she will decide this on their own after they have examined their conscience.

▶ forget that God is at the heart of everything, and that you can reach God via any route. It might be more engaging for a seven-year-old if you start by talking about, for example, his favourite action character, or what happened at school today, and then work around to the faith angle.

▶ worry if you cannot answer a question. If you admit to not knowing, that in itself is a way of teaching your grandchild that there are mysteries we cannot fully understand.

The teens

Our teenage years are when we question everything – from hairstyles and dress codes, to relationships, rules and matters of faith. Of course it is a natural part of growing up and becoming a new generation – but what a rollercoaster for everyone concerned! Family members can feel like helpless bystanders as the challenge of letting go intensifies and sex, pregnancy, smoking, alcohol and drugs become real and frightening possibilities. Even the most angelic child can suddenly appear possessed by demons and unfathomable preoccupations. Of course, not every family goes through this – but it is far from rare.

So if you are feeling out of your depth, here are a few pointers:

Do:

▶ understand that, deep down, even the most spiky, hostile and defensive teenager needs to be loved, cherished and held safe in the love of his or her family.

▶ be bold in bringing up anything that needs discussing, or inviting a troubled teenager to unburden themselves to you. Yes, you risk a tantrum or sullen rebuttal, but many teenagers feel they have nowhere to turn. Even if they do not seem responsive this time, they will know you are there for them.

▶ hone your listening skills for when they do want to talk.

▶ celebrate the generation gap rather than trying to minimise or disguise it. They will come to appreciate it as well.

▶ suggest that prayer will help.

Don't:

▶ be intimidated by a moody and morose grandchild.

▶ push your grandchild if he or she does not want to talk.

▶ jeopardise your privileged position if your grandchild wants to confide in you rather than his or her parents. Rise above status games and gently try to persuade your grandchild to talk to his or her parents, or you will further destabilise an already wobbly situation.

Confirmation

In asking to be confirmed, we are showing that we know, understand, and believe the faith of the Church. We are also showing that we wish to receive the gifts of the Spirit in order to take part in the Church's vocation of evangelisation.

But no matter how eager you are for your grandchild to experience the joys of "grown-up" faith, it must be their own choice. As well as receiving communion, a confirmed adult also has a responsibility to preach the Gospel – so pause for a moment to think what an awesome responsibility that is! If your grandchild says they want to wait, treat it as a sign of a thoughtful and mature approach and – treading gently – encourage concerned parents to do the same.

If your grandchild does decide to be confirmed, it is a wonderful opportunity to think afresh about your own confirmation and its significance for you, your spiritual life and your relationship with God.

Do:

▶ be honest. What has been your experience of the Holy Spirit and how have you preached the Gospel?

▶ find an opportunity to discuss it with your grandchild. You might find that it is an embarrassing subject for both of you, but a person who is to undergo the religious rite of confirmation should be able to get over any awkwardness and have an adult discussion – even with a family member!

Don't:

▶ feel you have to make your own experience sound rosy. Of course you do not want to be off-putting, but being confirmed is about making an informed choice, so you ought to be able to discuss it with your grandchild.

▶ judge yourself harshly if, in your soul-searching, you have to admit that you have not preached the Gospel or you have not knowingly allowed the Holy Spirit to influence you since your own confirmation. Make a confession and treat it as an opportunity to make a real change in your life.

> **"Like baptism, which it completes, confirmation is given only once, for it too imprints on the soul an _indelible spiritual mark_, the 'character', which is the sign that Jesus Christ has marked a Christian with the seal of his Spirit by clothing him with power from on high so that he may be his witness."**
>
> _Catechism of the Catholic Church_, 1304

Chapter four

Testing times

This section covers some aspects of family life that can prove particularly challenging for a grandmother.

Because all families and situations are different, it would be inappropriate to attempt to offer much practical advice in this limited space. Therefore, if you are really struggling, consider talking to a priest, counsellor or another grandmother. You could also contact one of the organisations listed at the back of this book. The key message is that you are not alone – there is support out there.

There is no such thing as constant harmony because life deals out so many challenges, stresses and suffering circumstances. In any family, members will experience sadness, chaos, conflict, anger and disunity.
But as a grandmother and a Christian, you are in a unique position to infuse even the bleakest situation with the all-encompassing love of God.

But just because something is covered here, it is not intended to imply that there is necessarily anything wrong with your family. For example, "distance" grandparenting is a challenge, but one that can motivate you to find fun and inventive ways to communicate with your grandchildren.

When your children don't share your faith

You know how much your faith means to you and how the sacraments have been defining markers in your life. When you experienced the death of someone close, for example, you may recall being held in the arms of the Church and the sacraments. Because of their huge importance and the cohesion they have given your life, you quite naturally did your utmost to ensure that your children had access to these signs of communion with God. You probably assumed that this would continue down the generations. So it can be heart-breaking when a parent sees their child move away from the Church, and even more painful when they do not pass Christian values on to their children. Do they not realise what they are missing out on? What if your grandchildren are not taught even the basics? What will they have to ground them in life? So many Catholic grandparents feel really thwarted, frustrated and muted by this situation.

You might have been asked explicitly not to teach the principal truths of Christianity to your grandchildren, or you might simply sense that the parents would not want it. But far too often, grandparents feel they have to tread softly around it, afraid to provoke a rumpus. Years of parenting might have taught you how to approach your own child, but he or she has divided loyalties now, and you do not know how their partner would react.

While it is often a tricky subject to broach, if you can possibly bring the subject up, DO! Ask what the boundaries are. Can you take the grandchildren to Mass once in a while? If not, do the parents mind you reading the Bible or saying prayers with them? It might sound like a clinical approach, but at least you will be clear about the parameters, and your own children will understand that you respect their wishes.

If you come away from the negotiation with empty hands, pray about any anger you may feel and remember that nobody can take your faith away from you. Also, nobody can stop you praying *for* your children and grandchildren, even if you cannot pray *with* them. And have faith – remember that God is always with your grandchildren, even if you cannot talk to them about it.

**A prayer
for perseverance**
Lord, who promised to be with us always, I bring before you [Names of the grandchildren]. I commit to live in such a way that your example shines through who I am, and what I do and say. I pray for [Names of parents] and ask you to guide them in their parenting. I pray for wisdom and grace to accept the situation.
Amen.

Ask Catherine

Jean writes:

Sunday was always a special family day when we were children. We always went to church, followed by a proper family lunch – a roast with all the trimmings. So I hate to think of our son Danny and his girlfriend Mel taking the kids to the supermarket on Sundays, followed by a burger and chips. Mel hates anything to do with religion, so I am walking on eggshells. Is there anything I can do or say?

"My granny is cool. She talks to God every day and she doesn't have a mobile phone."

Harry, age 10

Catherine replies:

Dear Jean,

I love a Sunday roast as much as anyone. However, at the risk of sounding unsympathetic, I think you need to separate faith from tradition and, indeed, from ideas about nutrition. A lot of people (and perhaps grandparents are particularly prone to this) become very attached to habits which, of themselves, have little or no intrinsic spiritual merit.

Jesus always met people where they were – the fishermen, tax collectors, sinners and sick people. How about joining the family one Sunday? If you are opposed to Sunday shopping you do not have to go to the supermarket. Perhaps you could suggest grace before the meal? That may be a step too far, given what you say about your son's girlfriend. So why not invite them round for a traditional Sunday lunch? Do not be intimidated by Mel's aversion to faith; in your own home you have every right to insist on saying grace. Even if that is all the religious instruction you are able to share with your grandchildren, have faith and patience. Our Lord is powerful enough to work through a simple prayer said together every now and again! My heartfelt prayers.

Catherine

Adoption or fostering

It is both wonderful and frightening how motherhood and grandmotherhood can rekindle emotions – some pure joy, others more difficult. If adoption has affected you in any way, for example, if you are adopted or your child is, do not be surprised if grandmotherhood stirs it all up again. Increasingly, those working in the field of adoption are recognising the importance of the extended family. So if you are struggling with any aspect of adoption, there are support agencies (see "Some useful contacts") that will be happy to talk it through. They can also suggest further counselling.

Mind the step

As we saw in the section on baptism, we have a tendency to be fiercely protective of our family – to the exclusion of all others. So the introduction of someone new into the family can feel like an intrusion, particularly when we feel we must treat them as family members. What is more, step-sons, -daughters, -grandsons, -granddaughters often become part of our family in the aftermath of death or divorce, when our strongest instinct is to retreat into our shells.

As ever, the appropriate organisation can offer support. In the meantime, there is an important, but difficult, passage in Mark's Gospel. It can be challenging to read if we interpret it as a rejection of Jesus' mother and siblings. However, if we read it with an open heart, it becomes clear that Jesus is in fact extending his definition of family to include the whole of humanity:

> "They said to him, 'Your mother and your brothers and sisters are outside, asking for you.' And he replied, 'Who are my mother and my brothers?' And looking at those who sat around him, he said, 'Here are my mother and my brothers! Whoever does the will of God is my brother and sister and mother.'"

Mark 3:32-35

When you don't feel the love

There is a lot of talk about the overwhelming love that a grandparent feels towards their grandchildren. But this is not true for everyone. The first thing to say is, that feeling – or not feeling – a certain way is not a sin in itself. Secondly, the chances are that your inability to connect emotionally with your grandchild is exacerbated by shame, frustration and a sense of duty to love. So try to accept how you *actually* feel, as opposed to how you think you *ought to* feel. Use reflective prayer, make a confession, or talk it through with a priest or counsellor. Lastly, we often relate to children better at different stages of their lives, so have faith and patience, and allow the relationship to develop organically, rather than trying to force anything.

When it ends in D.I.V.O.R.C.E or separation

This section assumes that your child is separating from his or her partner, but, of course, you might be affected in other ways by the breakdown of a relationship. Children are particularly sensitive to unrest and disharmony, so if it does happen in any branch of the family – for example, if you separate, or an uncle or aunt goes through divorce, be vigilant and watch out for the ripple effect. Be prepared for some tricky questions and try to find a way to answer them honestly, but in a way that children can understand.

To see how divorce affected Catherine Wiley's family, turn to chapter five.

It is not uncommon for couples to stare into the abyss at some point during their married life. So if you have been to the brink and back, you may find it exasperating if your child and his or her partner say they cannot work it out.

Through the Church we also learn that marriage is a covenanted communion for life between one man and one woman, so the fact that divorce flies in the face of this belief makes it doubly painful.

Do:

▶ everything possible to show your grandchildren unconditional love, without resorting to spoiling or over indulging them. Your role is to maintain constancy, which you will not be doing if your behaviour changes.

▶ take what you are told with a pinch of salt. The turmoil people go through during separation means they can feel a particular way one minute, and see things in a completely different light the next.

▶ be honest with yourself. Is part of you happy that the relationship has broken down? You certainly would not be the first grandmother to feel this way. Pray for wisdom, tolerance and fairness in your dealings with your former son- or daughter-in-law. After all, they remain the parent of your grandchild, no matter what.

▶ stay in touch with your ex son- or daughter-in-law, if at all possible.

▶ encourage your child to keep in regular contact with their ex and to allow access to the children, unless child safety is a real concern.

Don't:

▶ use it as an excuse to say "I told you so", or play the blame game. The breakdown of a relationship is very complex. Of course, as a grandparent you are an interested party, but at the same time you never know what goes on in another relationship.

▶ forget that the ripple effect of divorce lasts a lifetime – so stay vigilant! Your grandchild might need to talk about it at different stages of his or her life.

A death in the family

When experiencing grief, it can be agonisingly difficult to know how to express your sadness and possible rage. It is equally difficult to know how to support others in theirs and when to let grief take its course. Here are a few observations:

▶ It is common to feel helpless and out of your depth when someone is going through intense grief. So go easy on yourself, recognise your own sadness and try not to feel like a failure.

▶ Try to go easy on friends and family who fail to respond to your grief as you might expect or want.

▶ Sometimes the death of a loved one can bring consolation and peace. If you find yourself feeling that way, do not feel guilty or try to fight it.

▶ Recognise that people may be deeply distressed and not show it.

When a grandchild dies

Funeral arrangements can present Catholic grandparents with the supreme challenge of letting go. This can be exacerbated by the fact that non-Catholic or non-practising family members simply do not understand what you have been taught or your strength of feeling about it.

If you have concerns about how the funeral is being planned, it is a good idea to talk them through with a priest before confronting the parents. If you have not had much experience organising funerals, you may find it helpful to read up about it (see the "Further reading" section at the back of this book).

▶ Do not underestimate how traumatic miscarriage or abortion can be for everyone involved.

▶ In the case of a stillborn or unborn baby, it can help greatly if parents name the baby and arrange a funeral service with the local priest. Even when parents are adamantly opposed to religion, a non-religious ceremony may provide cohesion and focus at a time of great sadness.

▶ Above all, pray and keep praying.

Breda writes:

After a long battle with cancer, during which he had to have a leg amputated, my twelve-year-old grandson died two months ago.

I desperately want to be there for my son and daughter-in-law and for Luke's brother and sisters, but I find it hard just getting out of bed in the morning. I am worried that I do not have the strength or energy to support my family when they need me most.

Please help.

Catherine replies:

Dear **Breda**,

My heart goes out to you and your family. You sound exhausted and may possibly be suffering from depression. It is hardly surprising as you have been through years of pain and trauma. Of course your family needs you, but you have been there all these years. Now you need to take time for yourself. Only then will you be in a position to support anyone else. I would urge you to go to your doctor for medical help, and to your priest or a counsellor for emotional and spiritual help. God will take care of your family.

May God keep you united in love.

Catherine

"We know that the one who raised the Lord Jesus will raise us also with Jesus, and will bring us with you into his presence… So we do not lose heart. Even though our outer nature is wasting away, our inner nature is being renewed day by day."

2 Corinthians 4:14. 16

Challenging lifestyles

Nothing tests a parent's notions about morality quite the way children do, and that does not stop when children become parents themselves. Whatever you think about naturism, for example, it is one thing when it takes place on a beach in Spain, but quite another when you learn that your daughter and son-in-law intend to take their children on a nudist holiday. Equally, a grandmother who finds the idea of homosexuality difficult to accept is confronted by a whole new ethical challenge when her granddaughter comes out as gay and introduces her girlfriend.

Whatever your response to a real-life situation in your family, the worst thing you can do is try to force yourself to like or agree with it. That will only lead to inner conflict. You should also avoid, if possible, expressing your fierce disapproval, as this may drive a wedge between you and someone you love.

So how on earth can you learn to accept someone who has adopted a lifestyle of which you disapprove – particularly when it is something that affects your grandchildren? The answer, of course, depends very much on the individual circumstances; but here are some general suggestions:

Do:

▶ prayerfully remember that each and every one of us is made in the image and likeness of God.

▶ exercise tact and discretion when discussing the subject, especially when young children are around. However, do…

▶ … encourage an appropriate level of openness. A furtive atmosphere of family shame is unlikely to escape the attention of curious young minds.

Don't:

▶ feel you have to change your views. Think of open-mindedness in terms of loving the person, rather than agreeing with everything they do.

▶ dehumanise anyone. Remember that Jesus had no hesitation in approaching people whom others dehumanised and dismissed (Mark 2:15-17).

"God loves each of us as if there were only one of us."

St Augustine

A prayer for a grandchild with special needs:

Lord, as part of your creation, each of us is perfect. Thank you for the unique gift and enrichment that [Name] brings to our family and community. We pray for the strength and resources to be fully supportive, and the grace to love unconditionally.

Amen.

Special needs

Many grandmothers will remember children their own age who were "different" – and who were derided or mocked by their peers and, shamefully, sometimes even by adults. Thankfully special needs care and provision are much better nowadays.

Nevertheless, the birth of a child who needs specialist medical or educational help can present unique challenges for even the best-prepared, best-supported and most loving family.

One thing you can do, is remember (and remind parents) that the sacraments are available to everyone, no matter what the circumstances.

There are some fantastic resources available for catechists working with children who have special needs. It is always worth talking to a priest or catechist about how your grandchild can access these resources.

Do:

▶ find out as much as you can about your grandchild's condition.

▶ find and join a support group, and encourage parents to do the same.

Distance grandmotherhood

It is a safe bet that a large proportion of "silver surfers" – older people who regularly use the Internet – are grandmothers who live a distance from their grandchildren. It is a testament to the power of the grandmaternal bond that these women have overcome any reticence and reluctance to use new technology, and grasped the opportunity to stay in touch.

Just in case you have not already thought of them, here are a few ways that you can use technology to keep in touch with your grandchild:

▶ If your grandchild has a mobile phone, learn how to text and become a texting "gr&ma"!

▶ If you do not own a computer, get down to your local library or, funds allowing, invest in one. It does not have to be a super-fast, expensive model; a good, basic PC will have everything you need to start communicating.

▶ Become computer "conversant". There are plenty of classes aimed at helping people to get going. Expect to find it frustrating at times, but have faith that you will get the hang of it! Why not try…?

▷ Facebook (www.facebook.com). We hear horror stories about Facebook, but if it is used properly it can be a very powerful and effective way of staying in touch. Just be aware that youngsters often prefer to use this for peer communication only, so it is a good idea to check with your grandchild first – and, of course, make sure that parents are completely happy with it.

▷ Skype (www.skype.com) enables you to have face-to-face conversations with anyone who is also on Skype. It would not be suitable for use in a library, so you would need your own computer and you might need to invest in a webcam with a built-in microphone. However, most laptops nowadays come with a camera and microphone already installed.

"My friend Ruby doesn't have a granny so she's sharing with me."

Amber, age 7

40

If you are a confirmed "luddite" i.e. someone who fears "new" technology:

▶ Send your grandchild recorded messages. You could read a Bible story or say a prayer. If you are making an audio or video tape, check that the parents have a tape or video recorder to play them back.

▶ Phone regularly at a pre-arranged time so your grandchild can update you on their week.

Either way:

▶ Send postcards or cards addressed to each individual grandchild.

▶ NEVER forget a birthday.

▶ Celebrate the feast of Ss Joachim and Anne, Jesus' grandparents, on 26 July, by sending a card or saying a prayer over the phone.

A prayer to say with a child on the feast of Ss Joachim and Anne

Lord, who gave us Jesus as a baby, we thank you for giving him a loving family. We thank you especially for his grandparents, Joachim and Anne, and we remember grandparents everywhere. Amen.

"Grandchildren are the crown of the aged."

Proverbs 17:6

Chapter five

The art of being
a grandparent

by Catherine Wiley

As children, my nine brothers and sisters, and I were surrounded by people of faith and we took our faith for granted quite often – something that I, like so many grandparents today, cannot do for my own grandchildren. Even if a couple have achieved a happy marriage, are practising their faith, and have children who are baptised and preparing for the other sacraments, they will undoubtedly face external problems, such as the increasing secularisation of society, the influence of the media (particularly TV and the Internet), peer pressure, and so on.

The challenge and vocation of Catholic grandparents to pass on the faith to their grandchildren is joyful, creative and rewarding – but it is certainly not easy. That is why I call it an art. And, like any art, it takes practice, trial and error. I consider grandparents to be the natural evangelisers embedded in the heart of the family – and sometimes we need reminding of that!

I am a grandmother to ten beautiful grandchildren, including four step-grandchildren, of which some are not baptised. Some of my own children have fallen away from the faith and we have divorce in our family. Therefore, my husband and I are no strangers to the difficulties, challenges and heartache of modern-day Catholic family life. I meet many grandparents who spend a lot of their lives thinking that they are failures – and I feel that way myself more often than some might think. But, as a priest once said to me, "Failure is not an option". That is not to say that one will never do anything wrong. It means that our commitment to our grandchildren is lifelong. So, in a sense, there is no such thing as failure; we just carry on and learn from our mistakes.

The golden rule is to be a loving grandparent. With the love of Jesus that shines out of the Gospels, I firmly believe that you can overcome all the obstacles – some of which, I know, will appear insurmountable. But a grandmother is in the most powerful position of anyone to heal family rifts, and provide stability and constancy for grandchildren and their own children.

Central to the art of grandparenting is learning to let our children be the parents they need to be, while at the same time being confident grandparents. It is a delicate balance. On the one hand we want to be sensitive, thoughtful, unobtrusive, respectful and humble; while on the other hand we want to be fully present and able to be assertive when that is the appropriate way to be. After all, we want to be strong role models for our grandchildren, to enable them to grow into confident adults. Also, we want our faith to shine through, because that is who we are. Being a grandparent is certainly not about shrinking, being invisible or unheard.

I am a great believer in making the first move. But it often takes a bit of thought and prayer to work out the best approach. When I see that help is needed, I have learnt that it is generally better to phrase it as a question rather than a suggestion. So I will ask, "How can I help you with the grandchildren?"

Recently we had to have a family discussion – the first ever – because we realised that the grandchildren and step-grandchildren had started to squabble about who gets the most from us – the grandparents. Each of the families has different resources and lifestyles, so my husband and I felt that it was important to bring the matter into the open. We started by asking our children if any of them were having any problems, or if they needed anything. We took the discussion from there. I do not know if that was the best possible approach, but they were all calmer and happier afterwards. I think the fact that the subject was aired, and that we showed we cared, made a difference in itself – and it certainly helped the grandchildren.

If your children are not practising the faith, you cannot force them. That does not mean you have to hide your own faith. Some of the parents in our family do not go to Mass, but when the grandchildren come to stay with us, I take them to church. Having cleared it with their parents, it is non-negotiable – when you visit us, you go to Mass.

Another element of the art of grandparenting is to be there when you are needed – and not when you are not. Try not to be intrusive. It is amazing how many grandparents tell me that they pop round without making an arrangement. I always advise them to resist the urge, however strong, and to phone in advance. The last thing you want is to end up being resented or made to feel unwelcome.

It is important – health, time and finances permitting – to be there when you are needed. I know this can be difficult, especially if you live far away, lead a full life, or have other grandchildren. In order to maintain the constancy and stability that is so essential for your grandchildrens' wellbeing, grandparents cannot just drop in and drop out of their grandchildren's lives. A lot of planning is required to ensure regular contact – another very important skill in the art of grandparenting.

I will give you an example. One of my sons is divorced and because he struggles with addiction he is not able to see his four children very often. We see them as regularly as we possibly can, but it is not easy, particularly as our former daughter-in-law has moved to be nearer to her mother. This is some distance from where we live. It takes a lot of planning and can be very time-consuming, but we are determined to maintain the family link that our son is not always able to do. I know, for example, that we are having the grandchildren for half term in six months' time. This will help our son's ex-wife to plan a holiday. Whoever said the "third age" was all about taking it easy? This is one job from which you can never retire!

Through our experience of our son's divorce, as well as through the experiences of the many grandparents I meet, I know only too well that grandparents are the hidden victims of marriage breakdown, particularly when it is a son who is divorced or separated. Divorce in the family, no matter how old the children are, has far-reaching effects and can transcend generations. For instance, when our oldest grandchild comes to stay with us, he gets very homesick and misses his father. At times, I have found this especially difficult. He also misses his mother as well. We have learnt not to take it personally and to give him the little extra attention and reassurance that he needs. Thank God we have been able to do that, but it has not been easy by any means.

In addition, my former daughter-in-law is now engaged to be married again, and I believe there is a strong possibility that they will have another baby. We are very happy for her, although it brings up all sorts of issues for me as a grandmother. Where do I come into that scenario? What kind of relationship could I have with their child? How would I manage to integrate everyone? I cannot know until I meet the situation, but I do know that it is

important to keep the door open, to keep the communication going and to leave nobody out – and that means *nobody*! Always keep the love flowing and remember that a loving grandparent has a powerful influence!

That is easy to say, but modern family life can leave grandparents with a sense of being out of their depth. There are endless variations of what are known as "blended families" these days, and families composed of all sorts of people: from all kinds of backgrounds, of different persuasions, and living very different lifestyles. It makes family life very rich, but it can leave grandparents baffled, bemused and unsure how to set boundaries.

For example, I know two widowed grandparents who married each other. Of course that is something to celebrate, but there are potential pitfalls in this kind of scenario: children and grandchildren with torn loyalties, people not getting on as the grandparents might hope, and so on.

In my experience you do not have to withhold judgement. It all comes down to the golden rule – keeping the love of Jesus in your heart at all times. It takes patience, understanding and open communication for all the individuals in a blended family to really integrate. But by God's grace I have seen some extremely shaky beginnings turn into firm friendships and lasting family bonds!

In my work with the Catholic Grandparents' Association, I hear so many heart-rending stories about families torn apart by divorce, death, distance and prison. I know of grandparents who are unable to see their grandchildren because the granchildren are behind bars – just imagine how awful that must be!

One year, as some members of the Association were about to go on a pilgrimage, a grandmother I knew contacted me to let me know that she would not be able to attend, and she asked the group to pray for her and her family. She said, "Our only crime was that our son died five years ago, and we're not allowed to see our grandchildren. Over our garden fence, we can even hear them playing." Now of course there are two sides to every story and grief does terrible things to people – but how do you get over a situation like that? Is it even possible to talk about an "art" of grandparenting when a situation is so painful and raw? I really do not know the answer to that. But my advice is to pray and to never stop praying, because God knows all things and all will be well. Trust in him, particularly when you cannot trust yourself.

Although there are some very painful exceptions to the rule, I firmly believe that, when family breakdown occurs, grandparents are called to be an anchor for their bruised and hurting adult children. They also provide a source of support and stability for the little people whose world has fallen apart. None of this, of course, is unrelated to the fact that for many grandparents, faith is their anchor. It allows them to be the centre of stability, because they are secured by something far deeper than themselves.

I have also learnt that people and situations do change – often in very surprising ways. I can remember my own daughter, Francesca, aged around ten, wrapping herself around the trunk of a tree, determined not to go to Mass. I had to prise her fingernails out of the bark. Ironically, these days she is the most regular churchgoer of all my children, and she takes her two children to Mass every Sunday. It has been said that "patience is a virtue". It is also an aspect of the art of grandparenting!

Lastly, as well as being a grandparent, let us not forget that each of us is also a grandchild – even those of us who were not lucky enough to know our grandparents. As a grandchild, I knew only my maternal grandfather. I was one of ten children and he made me feel very special. I remember his great love for me and feeling safe in his care. It was from him that I heard my first Gospel story, and my first experience of prayer was at his knee, reciting the family Rosary. When he died, my siblings and I discovered that each of us thought we were his favourite! That, for me, sums up the extraordinary gift of grandparents.

Catherine's top tips

▶ Practise the art of being sensitive, thoughtful, unobtrusive, respectful and humble, without shrinking or hiding.

▶ Learn the art of being there when you are needed – but not when you are not.

▶ You will need to develop a thick skin – and that is an art form in itself!

▶ Sharpen your planning skills.

▶ Remember to keep the door open, keep the communication going and leave nobody out.

▶ Have faith that people and situations do change – by God's grace.

▶ Above all, practise the art of loving!

Chapter six

Conversations with
grandmothers

Yvonne is married to Chris. They have five children and six grandchildren, who range in age from one to fourteen.

We are a collection of individuals and all of us have very different perspectives on faith. In fact, in the family, only my daughter, Emily, and I are practising Catholics.

Although I do not want to preach or proselytise, I do not want to feel that faith is a no-go subject. So, recently, I found a quiet place to talk to each of my children separately, and I asked them, "How do you know that I am still a practising Christian?" I was moved to hear one of them say, "I know you always pray for us." However, I was not surprised by the strength of feeling from another, who told me that he did not want to have anything to do with the Catholic Church following the events and revelations of recent years.

One of my sons is married to a girl from a Methodist background, although she does not practise her faith. Surprisingly, however, I have noticed that he has started to take their young child to Mass. I know it is something he would rather just get on with, without feeling any pressure. Of course, I am interested to see what transpires, but for now it is important that he has his space.

It is interesting talking to Emily, who believes that it does not really matter who is a practising Catholic or who is not – the principles of Catholic social teaching are more important to her than belief or Mass attendance. Of course, part of me wishes that everyone knew Christ. However, it is also true that my children and grandchildren fill me with great pride. For me, they are a real gift from God – just as they are.

Colette is sixty-seven and married to Teddy. They have four children and eight grandchildren, who are aged between one and nine.

From the start, I absolutely loved being a mother. But, at first, I did find the prospect of becoming a grandmother daunting. I had little experience of grandmothers myself. As a child I only remember one grandmother, who lived in Liverpool. In those days she might as well have been on another planet. All in all, I probably met her about five times. Then, when my own children were born, my mother was suffering from debilitating rheumatoid arthritis, so, sadly, she was not able to be very involved in her grandchildren's lives. It makes me so thankful that my husband and I are both in good health.

I think one of the most important things a grandparent can do is to provide family cohesion and bring people together. For example, we try to go to Mass together, and sit together, and when we have a Sunday meal together, I like to make it a really special family time. It gives our children a chance to see one another and it is very important for the grandchildren to know each other as they grow up. We all went on holiday last year in Pembrokeshire. There were eighteen of us in total and it worked really well.

Every year, my husband and I also give each couple a break so they can go away together while we have the children to stay. So many couples spend years raising their children and leading busy lives; then they end up virtual strangers to one another. That is why we try to help our children to spend quality time with their spouses.

My husband and I know that we are very blessed to have our family, our resources and our health. For this reason we try to give thanks by taking our responsibility as grandparents very seriously. But it is not all serious – in fact, I would say that being a grandparent is one of the most enjoyable things I have ever done!

Kate is sixty-nine and married to Tony, also sixty-nine. They have three children: one son and two daughters, and four grandchildren, aged between six and seventeen.

I would say we are an ordinary Catholic family. Our children were educated at Catholic schools and they are baptised and confirmed in the Catholic faith. My husband and I have been involved in our parish and schools all our adult lives. All our children left the practice of their faith in their late teens. There was no pressure put on them to return, but two of them have returned as their circumstances have changed. These days, one daughter is practising and one comes and goes "on the threshold", while my son is not practising.

My son and one of my daughters married outside of the faith and, if I am honest, there was a certain sadness when that happened. But it has neither been allowed to sour family relationships, nor has it caused any difficulty in sharing my faith with my children or grandchildren. I am grateful to the Catholic Church for the way it has enriched my life and I believe that God loves everything that he creates, including my children. I believe also that what I have put into the children, in terms of Christian values, is still there. This is evident through their various struggles to live good lives and through their efforts to pass on Christian values to their children.

I share my faith obliquely and hope something will "stick" – I drop seeds and hope they will take root. I have strongly resisted the temptation to urge my children to get their babies baptised, make their First Communion, etc. I have done all the usual Catholic granny things in a bid to offer my grandchildren a hint of their Catholic heritage: Lent calendars, Advent calendars, wreaths and palm crosses (which the teenagers still look for if I am a little late!). They have all been given Christmas cribs and they find a large crib at my home every year at Christmas. Each new baby was given a baptism box with pictures of their birth and baptism, a candle with a note stating when it will be needed again, a certificate, a Bible, a prayer book and an icon of Our Lady of Perpetual Succour

(which still adorns bedroom walls). I have marked first communions and confirmation with collages of their lives, biblical references, gifts of the Holy Spirit, along with more worldly gifts like theatre tickets.

Aside from this, I have tried to create faith memories when the opportunity has arisen. One specific memory was of a holiday, during which my then seven-year-old grandson and I went to the local village church to explore. He and his sister are in the habit of phoning me to sing an Easter or Christmas song that they have learnt at school. This time, however, he had learnt the "moving on" song for the leavers at the end of the summer term. In the pulpit of the church he sang all fourteen verses to me, and he still remembers that as a "special" moment in Jesus' house.

My grandchildren have memories, too, of coming to Mass with me and my husband when they stayed, and singing with the choir in the choir-loft. More exciting still was the tour round the church and up the spiral staircase into the various mysterious nooks and crannies that make up God's house.

Recently, my grandson was the ring bearer at his aunt's (my daughter's) Catholic wedding. I explained to him the significance of the rings and that the rings symbolised the never-ending promise by the couple to love and remain faithful to each other. Also, I told him how important his role was – he was the person who brought these important symbols of promise to the happy couple. I hope this will be a lasting memory for my grandson.

During hard economic times, I alert the grandchildren to people in need in our towns. I do this by having a picture on the fridge door of Jesus feeding the five thousand. The logo of the local food bank and pictures of groceries are superimposed on the picture. It also has the biblical text underneath, "Give them something to eat" (Mark 6:37). It is great what can be done with a PC these days!

I have the Rembrandt picture of "The Return of the Prodigal Son" prominently displayed in the kitchen. It sits alongside a photo of my son cradling his newborn son on his shoulder. The hope is that comparisons will be made between Scripture stories and my son's life experience.

At Easter I have a "Resurrection Box" which the family opens over dinner. Everyone at the table is asked to bring something pertinent to a family member who is dead. This could be a memory, a piece of music, or even a photo. Then we talk about our deceased family members and the new life in the resurrection. Finally, we place the mementoes in the box.

Random conversations can sometimes create an opportunity to make a connection between Scripture and life. My family and I recently discussed the mystery of transubstantiation – how God turns bread and wine into the Body and Blood of Christ. We started by chatting about what happens when I eat the bread and drink the wine – I abide in Christ, and he in me. A revelation in a five-minute chat!

By God's grace, I think that all of this makes a difference to the lives of my children and grandchildren, and that they in turn will make a difference in their communities. My daughter-in-law told me that the children notice that partings are different with me – I always say "God Bless". In addition, my daughter informed me that her seventeen-year-old talks about the possibility of making decisions based on her faith beliefs; this is following conversations we have shared. This oldest grandchild, who is also "on the threshold" of faith and practice, is recognising how her Catholic heritage has been handed down to her and, I think, sees how much she would miss it if it were not so.

I believe that, in their families, my children are living the biblical stories. From time to time, they are the good shepherd, the vinedresser, the good Samaritan, or they are searching for a lost coin or sheep. If the opportunity arises I sometimes mention that they are living their lives biblically – and I see them glow! This may sound so sanctimonious! However, in reality it all happens very lightly.

I do not worry about my grandchildren and their faith, or lack of it. After all, as a friend often reminds me, "At some deep level, we are all safe in God's hands."

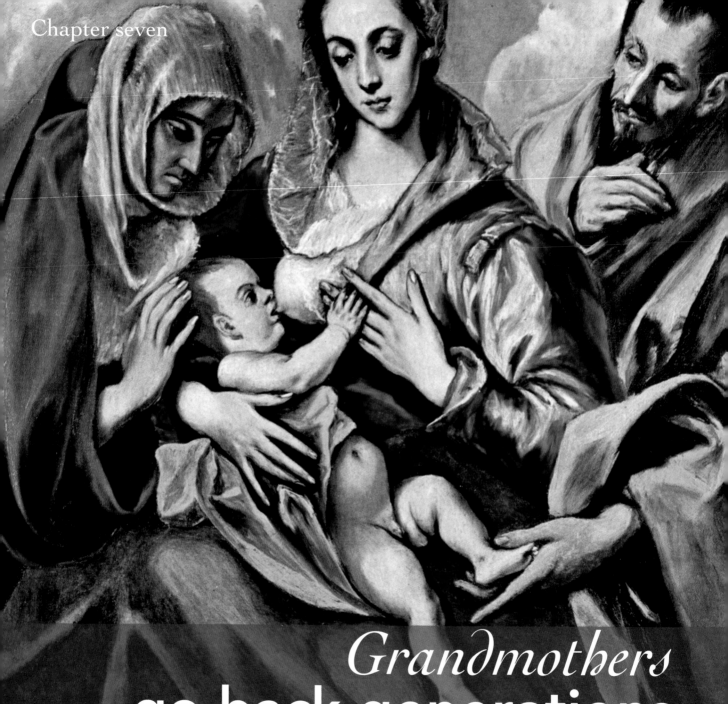

Chapter seven

Grandmothers
go back generations

There are resources within our faith tradition that can support grandmothers and which offer food for thought. Here are some examples of biblical grandmothers and their stories.

Jesus' Granny, by Denis McBride C.Ss.R.

When Matthew opens his Gospel he introduces us to a litany of Jesus' ancestors. It is as if Matthew hands us a photograph album of Jesus' relatives and says, "Before you meet Jesus, have a gander at the relatives." As in all families, the ancestral list includes a mixture of the good and the bad, the crooked and the cracked. Jesus does not come as a bolt from the blue: before he arrives, he belongs to a particular family, a particular people and a particular place. That is true, hopefully, of every child who is born.

Matthew does not mention Jesus' granny, St Anne. She is celebrated in the *Protoevangelium of James*, a second-century text purported to be written by James, the brother of the Lord. The narrative opens with Anna and Joachim lamenting their childlessness, but things soon change: "And, behold, an angel of the Lord stood by, saying, 'Anna, the Lord hath heard thy prayer, and thou shalt conceive, and shall bring forth; and thy seed shall be spoken of in all the world.'"

The narrative progresses, telling us that at the age of three Mary is taken to the Temple by her parents, where she stays until she is twelve years old. The priests now wonder what to do with her. The high priest prays and an angel appears, "And behold an angel of the Lord stood by him, saying unto him: 'Zacharias, go out and assemble the widowers of the people, and let them bring each his rod; and to whomsoever the Lord shall show a sign, his wife shall she be.'" The elderly widower, Joseph, is eventually chosen, after protesting he is an old man with a family already.

This Infancy Gospel first flourished in the East, promoting a great devotion to St Anne as the grandmother of Jesus, and a key figure in his formation. There was a ready recognition that Jesus belonged to a family that cared for and loved him, something that was hoped for in every family. Eventually the devotion was spread to the western world – from merchants and pilgrims, and crusaders from the Orient. St Anne, granny of Jesus, eventually arrived in the West to great acclaim in popular Catholic spirituality. As you can see from El Greco's painting, *Holy Family with St Anne*, (*opposite*), Granny Anne places her right hand gently on her grandson's head; Joseph cradles Jesus' left foot in his left hand and Mary offers her breast to her son, her eyes focusing on this little miracle. The family of three generations is celebrated – together, loving, attentive.

There is a magnificent and varied collection of paintings and statues from the mediaeval times of Jesus' granny as the protecting figure, both of Mary and Jesus. She unites them to the past, their historical root, and is ever present as a wise carer and advisor. As grandmother, she is utterly devoted to them all. She is a warm, gentle figure and an icon for all families.

Today St Anne is celebrated in a famous Redemptorist shrine, the beautiful Basilica of St Anne in Canada (*see right*). Its origins date back to 1658. Sainte- Anne-de-Beaupré, this great Catholic sanctuary in Quebec, is credited with many miracles from intercessions to St Anne. Jesus' granny, the one who petitioned God in her need, is now celebrated as the beloved grandmother in heaven who has time for everyone, particularly those in need of a kindly sensitive ear.

> "[Mary] was surrounded by the love and solicitude of her parents: Joachim and Anne. There she 'learned' from her mother, from St Anne, how to be a mother."
>
> John Paul II

Grandmothers in the bible

Naomi
step-grandmother of Obed

> "He shall be to you a restorer of life and a nourisher of your old age… Then Naomi took the child and laid him in her bosom, and became his nurse."
>
> Ruth 4:15-16

Naomi's story is told throughout the book of Ruth. After she is widowed and loses her two sons, she becomes extremely bitter in her bereavement. But her life is turned around by the gentle, insistent loyalty of her daughter-in-law, Ruth, who refuses to leave her side. When Ruth remarries Boaz and gives birth to a son, Obed (one of Jesus' ancestors), Naomi's friends are ecstatic for her. A couple of points arise from this story:

▶ Naomi is a prime example of how strong a bond can be, without necessarily being blood.

▶ When bad things happen, it is easy to become attached to negativity and, if we are not careful, it becomes our entrenched position. It would doubtless have taken real humility for Naomi to climb down and soften her stance towards Ruth – but it was infinitely worth it.

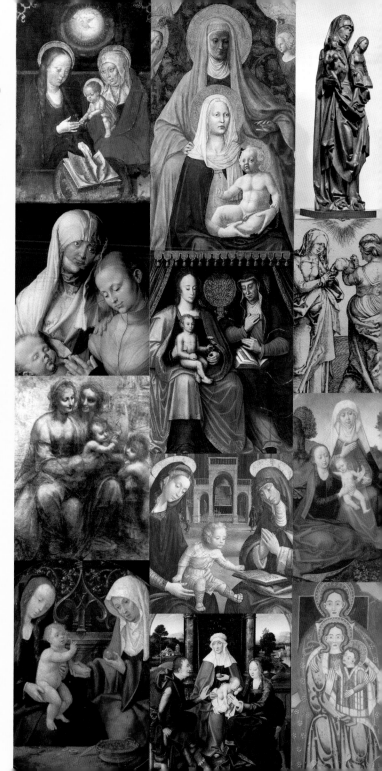

Hannah
grandmother of Joel and Abijah

"His sons did not follow in his ways, but turned aside after gain; they took bribes and perverted justice."

1 Samuel 8:3

After years of barrenness, Hannah promised God that if she had a child she would give it up to ministry. She conceived and bore Samuel, one of the great Hebrew prophets. When it came to the next generation, however, Joel and his brother Abijah, despite being given power, were corrupt and cruel. Hannah's story is interesting for anyone who thinks that devotion and piety will be repaid with devout and pious children and grandchildren.

Maacah
grandmother of Asa

"King Asa even removed his mother Maacah from being queen mother because she had made an abominable image for Asherah. Asa cut down her image, crushed it, and burned it."

2 Chronicles 15:16

Maacah is sometimes referred to as King Asa's mother – but in fact she was his grandmother (2 Chronicles 11:20). Her story may not have that much relevance for grandmothers today – other than to serve as a salutary warning that grandchildren do grow up, and sometimes even outgrow their grandparents in religious fervour!

Lois
grandmother of Timothy

"I am reminded of your sincere faith, a faith that lived first in your grandmother Lois and your mother Eunice and now, I am sure, lives in you. For this reason I remind you to rekindle the gift of God that is within you."

2 Timothy 1:5-6

This, put simply, is an example of a grandmother influencing her daughter, her grandson and, in turn, the entire history of the world. What power! Note Paul's choice of words: he does not write that she has passed it on by teaching or preaching – no, it is the faith that lives in her that has been her grandson's priceless inheritance.

"For the Lord is good; his steadfast love endures for ever, and his faithfulness to all generations."

Psalm 100:5

Chapter eight

To sum up

Hopefully you have learned from this book that you are *unique* and *wonderful*, as is your family situation. At the same time, it is also hoped that you have found that you share many things in common with other grandmothers.

The following is a summary of the important points touched on in the book:

Don't:

▶ take it personally

▶ take sides

▶ play status games

▶ be competitive with other grandparents

▶ fall into the trap of constantly thinking you are a failure as a grandmother

▶ give up, even when you have made a mistake

▶ forget the mistakes you made as a parent (but do not get hung up on them)

▶ ignore parents' wishes when it comes to the fundamental aspects of parenting – health and safety, education, teaching ethics, etc.

▶ try to find out from your grandchildren what goes on in their home

▶ criticise your child and his or her partner to your grandchildren

▶ forget to look after your own needs and take it easy – eat well, rest well and you will have enough energy to play well!

Never:

▶ forcibly pass on the faith to your grandchild if his or her parents have told you not to

▶ do anything to cut off communication

Do:

- ▶ think of grandparenting as an ongoing commitment and challenge, and learn to embrace it as such
- ▶ aim to be a friend and ally to your grandchildren, without alienating parents
- ▶ continually practise and pray about the art of letting go. See it as a positive rather than a negative
- ▶ hone your listening skills
- ▶ allow parents to make mistakes – it is how you learned
- ▶ count to a hundred before offering advice or guidance to parents. Are you sure there is no hidden agenda on your part? What do you really want to achieve and are you going the best way about it?
- ▶ show unconditional love to your grandchildren, even when you have to reprimand them
- ▶ talk to other grandparents about their experiences, and share your own
- ▶ be humble in learning from your grandchildren's example – remember that "a little child shall lead them" (Isaiah 11:6)

Always:

- ▶ ensure that parents are happy with any religious teaching you give your grandchild
- ▶ make sure that your child and their partner know that you want to support them as parents

Above all, always be a loving grandmother.

A prayer for a *loving grandmother*

Lord, thank you
for the rhythm of life.
I pray for all my family,
past and present:
[pause here to pray for individuals].
As I continue my journey
as a follower of Christ,
I commit to passing on my
faith to new generations.
Amen.

SOME USEFUL CONTACTS

Support for grandparents

Catholic Grandparents' Association
www.catholicgrandparentsassociation.org
Tel. 00 353 (0)98 24877

The Grandparents' Association
www.grandparents-association.org.uk
Tel. 0845 434 9585

Grandparents Plus
www.grandparentsplus.org.uk
Tel. 0300 123 7015

Grannynet
www.grannynet.co.uk

Grandparents Apart UK
www.grandparentsapart.co.uk
Tel. 0141 882 5658

Support for families

Care for the Family
www.careforthefamily.org.uk
Tel. 029 2081 0800

Safety in the home

Royal Society for the Prevention of Accidents
www.rospa.com
Tel. 0121 248 2000

Child Accident Prevention Trust
www.capt.org.uk
Tel. 020 7608 3828

Adoption support & counselling

Adoption UK
www.adoptionuk.org
Tel. 0844 848 7900

After Adoption
www.afteradoption.org.uk
Tel. 0800 0 568 578

Redemptorist Publications is not responsible for the content of external internet sites.

FURTHER READING

Redemptorist Publications has published a series of books on the sacraments, along with a wealth of resources for families and children. They include:

Your Baby's Baptism

Your Child's First Confession

Your Child's First Communion

Your Wedding: a Guide to Getting Married in the Catholic Church

A Catholic Funeral: a Guide for the Family

How to Survive Being Married to a Catholic

I Belong Special

To order your copy of any of these titles, simply phone 01420 88222 or email sales@rpbooks.co.uk, or you can order online at www.rpbooks.co.uk.

Dear Lord, isn't she just the wee dote?

And I still have my earrings intact!

Being a grandmother is such a blessing,
since you don't have to do anything but be yourself.
The best time of my life is looking after Jackie,
and I can give her my undivided attention
and play daft games and sing silly songs –
and always offer a listening ear. Neither of us
is in a hurry, longing to be away somewhere else:
we don't have to squeeze each other into diaries.

As a Catholic granny I do have one wee worry –
the old biblical one: "What will this child turn out to be?"
Jackie's parents are "resting Catholics" –
having a bit of a break, they say, from organised religion.
They're wonderful people and loving parents,
and they did have Jackie baptised, though it stopped there.

I see grandmothers as the keepers of family history,
guiding lights to safe havens in these foggy times.
I've been teaching Jackie about you, Lord,
teaching her how to pray. Give her an attentive ear,
and let her know she is loved beyond the reaches
of our family, our history, this time, this world.

Let her know that she is not just our child but your child,
a child of God, dreamed from the foundation of the world.

Denis McBride C.Ss.R.,
Praying with Pictures